Poems of Creatures Large and Small

Poems of Creatures Large and Small

Edited by Gail Harvey

AVENEL BOOKS
New York

Introduction and Compilation
Copyright © 1991 by Outlet Book Company, Inc.
All rights reserved
First published in 1991 by Avenel Books
distributed by Outlet Book Company, Inc.,
a Random House Company,
225 Park Avenue South
New York, New York 10003

Manufactured in Singapore

Designed by Melissa Ring

Library of Congress Cataloging-in-Publication Data
Poems of creatures, large and small / edited by Gail
Harvey.
    p.   cm.
  ISBN 0-517-05324-1
  1. Animals—Poetry.   2. Poetry—Collections.
  I. Harvey, Gail.
PN6110.A7P64   1990
808.81'936—dc20   90-45120
                                          CIP

8   7   6   5   4   3   2   1

Contents

SONNET TO A CAT

*C*at! who hast pass'd thy grand climacteric,
 How many mice and rats hast in thy days
 Destroy'd?—How many tit bits stolen? Gaze
With those bright languid segments green, and prick
Those velvet ears—but pr'ythee do not stick
 Thy latent talons in me—and upraise
 Thy gentle mew—and tell me all thy frays
Of fish and mice, and rats and tender chick.
Nay, look not down, nor lick thy dainty wrists—
 For all the wheezy asthma,—and for all
Thy tail's tip is nick'd off—and though the fists
 Of many a maid have given thee many a maul,
Still is that fur as soft as when the lists
 In youth thou enter'dst on glass bottled wall.

JOHN KEATS

TO MY DOG "BLANCO"

*M*y dear, dumb friend, low lying there,
A willing vassal at my feet,
Glad partner of my home and fare,
My shadow in the street,

I look into your great brown eyes,
Where love and loyal homage shine,
And wonder where the difference lies
Between your soul and mine!

For all of good that I have found
Within myself or human kind,
Hath royally informed and crowned
Your gentle heart and mind.

I scan the whole broad earth around
For that one heart which, leal and true,
Bears friendship without end or bound,
And find the prize in you.

I trust you as I trust the stars;
Nor cruel loss, nor scoff of pride,
Nor beggary, nor dungeon bars,
Can move you from my side!

As patient under injury
As any Christian saint of old,
As gentle as a lamb with me,
But with your brothers bold.

More playful than a frolic boy,
More watchful than a sentinel,
By day and night your constant joy
To guard and please me well,

I clasp your head upon my breast—
The while you whine and lick my hand—
And thus our friendship is confessed,
And thus we understand!

Ah, Blanco! did I worship God
As truly as you worship me,
Or follow where my Master trod
With your humility,

Did I sit fondly at His feet,
As you, dear Blanco, sit at mine,
And watch Him with a love as sweet,
My life would grow divine!

JOSIAH GILBERT HOLLAND

EPITAPH TO A DOG

*Lord Byron's tribute to "Boatswain," on a monument
in the garden of Newstead Abbey.*

*N*ear this spot
Are deposited the Remains
of one
Who possessed Beauty
Without Vanity,
Strength without Insolence,
Courage without Ferocity,
And all the Virtues of Man
Without his Vices.

This Praise, which would be unmeaning flattery
If inscribed over Human Ashes,
Is but a just tribute to the Memory of
"Boatswain," a Dog
Who was born at Newfoundland,
May, 1803,
And died at Newstead Abbey
Nov. 18, 1808.

When some proud son of man returns to earth,
Unknown to glory, but upheld by birth,
The sculptor's art exhausts the pomp of woe,
And storied urns record who rests below.
When all is done, upon the tomb is seen,
Not what he was, but what he should have been.
But the poor dog, in life the firmest friend,
The first to welcome, foremost to defend,
Whose honest heart is still his master's own,
Who labors, fights, lives, breathes for him alone,
Unhonored falls, unnoticed all his worth,
Denied in heaven the soul he held on earth—
While man, vain insect! hopes to be forgiven,
And claims himself a sole exclusive heaven.
Oh man! thou feeble tenant of an hour,
Debased by slavery, or corrupt by power—
Who knows thee well must quit thee with disgust,
Degraded mass of animated dust!
Thy love is lust, thy friendship all a cheat,
Thy smiles hypocrisy, thy words deceit!
By nature vile, ennobled but by name,
Each kindred brute might bid thee blush for shame.

Ye, who perchance behold this simple urn,
Pass on—it honors none you wish to mourn.
To mark a friend's remains these stones arise;
I never knew but one—and here he lies.

GEORGE GORDON, LORD BYRON

FLUSH OR FAUNUS

*Y*ou see this dog. It was but yesterday
I mused forgetful of his presence here
Till thought on thought drew downward tear on tear,
When from the pillow where wet-cheeked I lay,
A head as hairy as Faunus thrust its way
Right sudden against my face,—two golden-clear
Great eyes astonished mine,—a drooping ear
Did flap me on either cheek to dry the spray!
I started first as some Arcadian
Amazed by goatly god in twilight grove,
But as the bearded vision closelier ran
My tears off, I knew Flush, and rose above
Surprise and sadness,—thanking the true Pan
Who, by low creatures, leads to heights of love.

ELIZABETH BARRETT BROWNING

THE COW

*T*he friendly cow all red and white,
   I love with all my heart:
She gives me cream with all her might,
   To eat with apple tart.

She wanders lowing here and there,
   And yet she cannot stray,
All in the pleasant open air,
   The pleasant light of day;

And blown by all the winds that pass
   And wet with all the showers,
She walks among the meadow grass
   And eats the meadow flowers.

ROBERT LOUIS STEVENSON

LAMBS AT PLAY

Say, ye that know, ye who have felt and seen
Spring's morning smiles, and soul-enlivening green,—
Say, did you give the thrilling transport way,
Did your eye brighten, when young lambs at play
Leaped o'er your path with animated pride,
Or gazed in merry clusters by your side?
Ye who can smile—to wisdom no disgrace—
At the arch meaning of a kitten's face;
If spotless innocence and infant mirth
Excites to praise, or gives reflection birth;
In shades like these pursue your favorite joy,
Midst nature's revels, sports that never cloy.
A few begin a short but vigorous race,
And indolence, abashed, soon flies the place:
Thus challenged forth, see thither, one by one,
From every side, assembling playmates run;
A thousand wily antics mark their stay,
A starting crowd, impatient of delay;
Like the fond dove from fearful prison freed,
Each seems to say, "Come, let us try our speed";
Away they scour, impetuous, ardent, strong,
The green turf trembling as they bound along
Adown the slope, then up the hillock climb,
Where every mole-hill is a bed of thyme,
Then, panting, stop; yet scarcely can refrain,
A bird, a leaf, will set them off again:
Or, if a gale with strength unusual blow,
Scattering the wild-brier roses into snow,
Their little limbs increasing efforts try;
Like the torn flower, the fair assemblage fly.
Ah, fallen rose! sad emblem of their doom;
Frail as thyself, they perish while they bloom!

ROBERT BLOOMFIELD

BLACK SHEEP

*F*rom their folded tents they wander far,
    Their ways seem harsh and wild;
They follow the beck of a baleful star,
    Their paths are dream beguiled.
Yet haply they sought but a wilder range,
    Some loftier mountain slope,
And little recked of the country strange
    Beyond the gates of hope.

And haply a bell with a luring call
    Summoned their feet to tread
Midst the cruel rocks where the deep pitfall
    And the lurking snare are spread.
May be in spite of tameless days
    Of outcast liberty,
They're sick at heart for the homely ways
    Where their garnered brothers be.

And oft at night when the plains fall dark,
    And the hills loom large and dim;
For the Shepherd's voice they mutely hark,
    And their souls go out to him.
Meanwhile, Black Sheep! Black Sheep! we cry,
    Safe in the inner fold;
And may be they hear and wonder why,
    And marvel, out in the cold.

RICHARD BURTON

THE ARAB'S FAREWELL TO HIS HORSE

*M*y beautiful! my beautiful! that standest meekly by,
With thy proudly arch'd and glossy neck, and dark and
      fiery eye,
Fret not to roam the desert now, with all thy
      wingèd speed;
I may not mount on thee again,—thou'rt sold,
      my Arab steed!
Fret not with that impatient hoof,—snuff not the
      breezy wind,—
The farther that thou fliest now, so far am I behind:
The stranger hath thy bridle-rein,—thy master hath
      his gold,—
Fleet-limb'd and beautiful, farewell; thou'rt sold,
      my steed, thou'rt sold.

Farewell! those free, untired limbs full many a mile
      must roam,
To reach the chill and wintry sky which clouds the
      stranger's home;
Some other hand, less fond, must now thy corn and
      bread prepare,

The silky mane I braided once, must be another's care!
The morning sun shall dawn again, but never more
             with thee
Shall I gallop through the desert paths, where we were
             wont to be;
Evening shall darken on the earth, and o'er the
             sandy plain
Some other steed, with slower step, shall bear me home again.

Yes, thou must go! the wild, free breeze, the brilliant
             sun and sky,
Thy master's home,—from all of these my exiled one
             must fly;
Thy proud dark eye will grow less proud, thy step
             become less fleet,
And vainly shalt thou arch thy neck, thy master's hand
             to meet.
Only in sleep shall I behold that dark eye, glancing
             bright;—
Only in sleep shall hear again that step so firm and light;
And when I raise my dreaming arm to check or cheer
             thy speed,
Then must I, starting, wake to feel—thou'rt *sold,*
             my Arab steed!

Ah! rudely, then, unseen by me, some cruel hand may chide,
Till foam-wreaths lie, like crested waves, along thy
             panting side:
And the rich blood that's in thee swells, in thy indignant
             pain,
Till careless eyes, which rest on thee, may count each
             started vein.
Will they ill use thee? If I thought—but no, it cannot be,—
Thou art so swift, yet easy curb'd; so gentle, yet so free;
And yet, if haply, when thou'rt gone, my lonely heart
             should yearn,—
Can the hand which casts thee from it now command
             thee to return?

Return! alas! my Arab steed! what shall thy master do,
When thou, who wast his all of joy, hast vanish'd from
his view?
When the dim distance cheats mine eye, and through
the gathering tears,
Thy bright form, for a moment, like the false mirage
appears;
Slow and unmounted shall I roam, with weary step
alone,
Where, with fleet step and joyous bound, thou oft hast
borne me on;
And sitting down by that green well, I'll pause and
sadly think,
"It was here he bow'd his glossy neck when last I saw
him drink!"

When last I saw thee drink!—Away! the fever'd dream
is o'er,—
I could not live a day, and *know* that we should meet
no more!
They tempted me, my beautiful!—for hunger's power
is strong,—
They tempted me, my beautiful! but I have loved too
long.
Who said that I had given thee up? who said that thou
wast sold?
'Tis false,—'tis false! my Arab steed! I fling them back
their gold!
Thus, *thus,* I leap upon thy back, and scour the distant
plains;
Away! who overtakes us now shall claim thee for his
pains!

CAROLINE NORTON

TO A MOUSE

On turning her up in her nest with the plough.
November, 1785

*W*ee, sleekit, cow'rin', tim'rous beastie,
O, what a panic 's in thy breastie!
Thou need na start awa' sae hasty,
    Wi' bickering brattle!
I wad be laith to rin an' chase thee,
    Wi' murd'ring pattle!

I'm truly sorry man's dominion
Has broken nature's social union,
An' justifies that ill opinion
    Which makes thee startle
At me, thy poor earth-born companion,
    An' fellow-mortal!

I doubt na, whyles, but thou may thieve;
What then? poor beastie, thou maun live!
A daimen icker in a thrave
    'S a sma' request;
I'll get a blessin' wi' the laive,
    And never miss 't!

Thy wee bit housie, too, in ruin!
Its silly wa's the win's are strewin'!
As naething now to big a new ane
    O' foggage green!
An' bleak December's winds ensuin',
    Baith snell and keen!

Thou saw the fields laid bare an' waste,
An' weary winter comin' fast,
An' cozie here, beneath the blast,
        Thou thought to dwell,
Till, crash! the cruel coulter past
        Out through thy cell.

That wee bit heap o' leaves an' stibble
Has cost thee mony a weary nibble!
Now thou's turned out for a' thy trouble,
        But house or hald,
To thole the winter's sleety dribble,
        An' cranreuch cauld!

But, Mousie, thou art no thy lane,
In proving foresight may be vain:
The best-laid schemes o' mice an' men
        Gang aft a-gley,
An' lea'e us naught but grief and pain,
        For promised joy.

Still thou art blest, compared wi' me!
The present only toucheth thee:
But, och! I backward cast my e'e
        On prospects drear;
An' forward, though I canna see,
        I guess an' fear.

ROBERT BURNS

BATTLE BUNNY

"After the men were ordered to lie down, a white rabbit, which had been hopping hither and thither over the field swept by grape and musketry, took refuge among the skirmishers, in the breast of a corporal."—Report of the Battle of Malvern Hill, 1864.

*B*unny, lying in the grass,
Saw the shining column pass;
Saw the starry banner fly,
Saw the chargers fret and fume,
Saw the flapping hat and plume—
Saw them with his moist and shy
Most unspeculative eye,
Thinking only, in the dew,
That it was a fine review—
Till a flash, not all of steel,
Where the rolling caissons wheel,
Brought a rumble and a roar
Rolling down that velvet floor,
And like blows of autumn flail
Sharply threshed the iron hail.

Bunny, thrilled by unknown fears,
Raised his soft and pointed ears,
Mumbled his prehensile lip,
Quivered his pulsating hip,
As the sharp vindictive yell
Rose above the screaming shell;
Thought the world and all its men—
All the charging squadrons meant—
All were rabbit-hunters then,
All to capture him intent.
Bunny was not much to blame:
Wiser folk have thought the same—
Wiser folk who think they spy
Every ill begins with "I."

Wildly panting here and there,
Bunny sought the freer air,
Till he hopped below the hill,
And saw, lying close and still,
Men with muskets in their hands.
(Never Bunny understands
That hypocrisy of sleep,
In the vigils grim they keep,
As recumbent on that spot
They elude the level shot.)

One—a grave and quiet man,
Thinking of his wife and child
Far beyond the Rapidan,
Where the Androsaggin smiled—
Felt the little rabbit creep,
Nestling by his arm and side,
Wakened from strategic sleep,
To that soft appeal replied,
Drew him to his blackened breast,
And—
        But you have guessed the rest.
Softly o'er that chosen pair
Omnipresent Love and Care
Drew a mightier Hand and Arm,
Shielding them from every harm;
Right and left the bullets waved,
Saved the savior for the saved.

Who believes that equal grace
God extends in every place,
Little difference he scans
'Twixt a rabbit's God and man's.

BRET HARTE

A MOTH

A clumsy clot of shadow in the fold
  Of the white blind,—a moth asleep or dead,
And hooked therein with still, tenacious hold,
  And dusky vans outspread.

Laid on my hand a wonder of dull dyes,
  A somber miracle of mingled grain,
Gray etched on gray, faint as faint memories,
  Dim stain invading stain.

Each wing-edge scalloped clear as any shell's,
  With rippled repetitions ebbing in
Rhyme within rhyme, as when cathedral bells
  Remit their joyous din.

Complete is it of broken laceries,
  A pencilled maze of blending grays,
Mosaic of symmetric traceries,
  Assorted in sweet ways.

Black velvet grainings upon pearly ash,
  An elf-wrought broidery of hues they stole
From the black moss-blot, and the lichen-splash,
  From birch or beechen bole.

Strange-headed thing, in ruminative rest
  Stirring its flexile antlers dreamily,
With great ghoul-eyes and sable-feathered breast,
  In sleep's security.

"There rest thee, and sleep off thy drowsy fit,
  Till night shall triumph in the dusky glades,
And mass her conquering glooms, then rise and flit—
  A shadow through the shades!"

Henry Bellyse Baildon

THE BUTTERFLY'S DAY

*F*rom cocoon forth a butterfly
As lady from her door
Emerged—a summer afternoon—
Repairing everywhere,

Without design, that I could trace,
Except to stray abroad
On miscellaneous enterprise
The clovers understood.

Her pretty parasol was seen
Contracting in a field
Where men made hay, then struggling hard
With an opposing cloud,

Where parties, phantom as herself,
To Nowhere seemed to go
In purposeless circumference,
As 't were a tropic show.

And notwithstanding bee that worked,
And flower that zealous blew,
This audience of idleness
Disdained them, from the sky,

Till sundown crept, a steady tide,
And men that made the hay,
And afternoon, and butterfly,
Extinguished in its sea.

EMILY DICKINSON

A NOISELESS, PATIENT SPIDER

A noiseless, patient spider,
I marked, where, on a little promontory,
    it stood isolated;
Marked how, to explore the vacant, vast surrounding,
It launched forth filament, filament, filament,
    out of itself;
Ever unreeling them—ever tirelessly speeding them.

And you, O my Soul, where you stand,
Surrounded, surrounded, in measureless oceans of space,
Ceaselessly musing, venturing, throwing,—seeking the
        spheres, to connect them;
Till the bridge you will need, be formed—
        till the ductile anchor hold;
Till the gossamer thread you fling, catch somewhere,
        O my Soul.

WALT WHITMAN

THE CRICKET

*L*ittle inmate, full of mirth,
Chirping on my kitchen hearth,
Wheresoe'er be thine abode
Always harbinger of good,
Pay me for thy warm retreat
With a song more soft and sweet;
In return thou shalt receive
Such a strain as I can give.

Thus thy praise shall be expressed,
Inoffensive, welcome guest!
While the rat is on the scout,
And the mouse with curious snout,
With what vermin else infest
Every dish, and spoil the best;
Frisking thus before the fire,
Thou hast all thy heart's desire.

Though in voice and shape they be
Formed as if akin to thee,
Thou surpassest, happier far,
Happiest grasshoppers that are;
Theirs is but a summer's song,
Thine endures the winter long,
Unimpaired, and shrill, and clear,
Melody throughout the year.

Neither night nor dawn of day
Puts a period to thy play:
Sing then—and extend thy span
Far beyond the date of man;
Wretched man, whose years are spent
In repining discontent,
Lives not, aged though he be,
Half a span, compared with thee.

WILLIAM COWPER

TO AN INSECT

I love to hear thine earnest voice,
  Wherever thou art hid,
Thou testy little dogmatist,
  Thou pretty Katydid!
Thou mindest me of gentlefolks,—
  Old gentlefolks are they,—
Thou say'st an undisputed thing
  In such a solemn way.

Thou art a female, Katydid!
  I know it by the trill
That quivers through thy piercing notes,
  So petulant and shrill;
I think there is a knot of you
  Beneath the hollow tree,—
A knot of spinster Katydids,—
  Do Katydids drink tea?

O tell me where did Katy live,
  And what did Katy do?
And was she very fair and young,
  And yet so wicked, too?
Did Katy love a naughty man,
  Or kiss more cheeks than one?
I warrant Katy did no more
  Than many a Kate has done.

THE CRICKET

Little inmate, full of mirth,
Chirping on my kitchen hearth,
Wheresoe'er be thine abode
Always harbinger of good,
Pay me for thy warm retreat
With a song more soft and sweet;
In return thou shalt receive
Such a strain as I can give.

Thus thy praise shall be expressed,
Inoffensive, welcome guest!
While the rat is on the scout,
And the mouse with curious snout,
With what vermin else infest
Every dish, and spoil the best;
Frisking thus before the fire,
Thou hast all thy heart's desire.

Though in voice and shape they be
Formed as if akin to thee,
Thou surpassest, happier far,
Happiest grasshoppers that are;
Theirs is but a summer's song,
Thine endures the winter long,
Unimpaired, and shrill, and clear,
Melody throughout the year.

Neither night nor dawn of day
Puts a period to thy play:
Sing then—and extend thy span
Far beyond the date of man;
Wretched man, whose years are spent
In repining discontent,
Lives not, aged though he be,
Half a span, compared with thee.

WILLIAM COWPER

TO AN INSECT

I love to hear thine earnest voice,
   Wherever thou art hid,
Thou testy little dogmatist,
   Thou pretty Katydid!
Thou mindest me of gentlefolks,—
   Old gentlefolks are they,—
Thou say'st an undisputed thing
   In such a solemn way.

Thou art a female, Katydid!
   I know it by the trill
That quivers through thy piercing notes,
   So petulant and shrill;
I think there is a knot of you
   Beneath the hollow tree,—
A knot of spinster Katydids,—
   Do Katydids drink tea?

O tell me where did Katy live,
   And what did Katy do?
And was she very fair and young,
   And yet so wicked, too?
Did Katy love a naughty man,
   Or kiss more cheeks than one?
I warrant Katy did no more
   Than many a Kate has done.

THE CRICKET

Little inmate, full of mirth,
Chirping on my kitchen hearth,
Wheresoe'er be thine abode
Always harbinger of good,
Pay me for thy warm retreat
With a song more soft and sweet;
In return thou shalt receive
Such a strain as I can give.

Thus thy praise shall be expressed,
Inoffensive, welcome guest!
While the rat is on the scout,
And the mouse with curious snout,
With what vermin else infest
Every dish, and spoil the best;
Frisking thus before the fire,
Thou hast all thy heart's desire.

Though in voice and shape they be
Formed as if akin to thee,
Thou surpassest, happier far,
Happiest grasshoppers that are;
Theirs is but a summer's song,
Thine endures the winter long,
Unimpaired, and shrill, and clear,
Melody throughout the year.

Neither night nor dawn of day
Puts a period to thy play:
Sing then—and extend thy span
Far beyond the date of man;
Wretched man, whose years are spent
In repining discontent,
Lives not, aged though he be,
Half a span, compared with thee.

WILLIAM COWPER

THE BEE

*L*ike trains of cars on tracks of plush
I hear the level bee:
A jar across the flowers goes,
Their velvet masonry

Withstands until the sweet assault
Their chivalry consumes,
While he, victorious, tilts away
To vanquish other blooms.

His feet are shod with gauze,
His helmet is of gold;
His breast, a single onyx
With chrysoprase, inlaid.

His labor is a chant,
His idleness a tune;
Oh, for a bee's experience
Of clovers and of noon!

EMILY DICKINSON

THE FLY

*L*ittle fly,
Thy summer's play
My thoughtless hand
Has brush'd away.

Am not I
A fly like thee?
Or art not thou
A man like me?

For I dance,
And drink, & sing;
Till some blind hand
Shall brush my wing.

If thought is life
And strength & breath,
And the want
Of thought is death;

Then am I
A happy fly,
If I live
Or if I die.

WILLIAM BLAKE

TO AN INSECT

I love to hear thine earnest voice,
  Wherever thou art hid,
Thou testy little dogmatist,
  Thou pretty Katydid!
Thou mindest me of gentlefolks,—
  Old gentlefolks are they,—
Thou say'st an undisputed thing
  In such a solemn way.

Thou art a female, Katydid!
  I know it by the trill
That quivers through thy piercing notes,
  So petulant and shrill;
I think there is a knot of you
  Beneath the hollow tree,—
A knot of spinster Katydids,—
  Do Katydids drink tea?

O tell me where did Katy live,
  And what did Katy do?
And was she very fair and young,
  And yet so wicked, too?
Did Katy love a naughty man,
  Or kiss more cheeks than one?
I warrant Katy did no more
  Than many a Kate has done.

Dear me! I'll tell you all about
   My fuss with little Jane,
And Ann, with whom I used to walk
   So often down the lane,
And all that tore their locks of black,
   Or wet their eyes of blue,—
Pray tell me, sweetest Katydid,
   What did poor Katy do?

Ah no! the living oak shall crash,
   That stood for ages still,
The rock shall rend its mossy base
   And thunder down the hill,
Before the little Katydid
   Shall add one word, to tell
The mystic story of the maid
   Whose name she knows so well.

Peace to the ever-murmuring race!
   And when the latest one
Shall fold in death her feeble wings
   Beneath the autumn sun,
Then shall she raise her fainting voice,
   And lift her drooping lid,
And then the child of future years
   Shall hear what Katy did.

OLIVER WENDELL HOLMES

COYOTE

*B*lown out of the prairie in twilight and dew,
Half bold and half timid, yet lazy all through;
Loath ever to leave, and yet fearful to stay,
He limps in the clearing, an outcast in gray.

A shade on the stubble, a ghost by the wall,
Now leaping, now limping, now risking a fall,
Lop-eared and large jointed, but ever alway
A thoroughly vagabond outcast in gray.

Here, Carlo, old fellow,—he's one of your kind,—
Go, seek him, and bring him in out of the wind.
What! snarling, my Carlo! So even dogs may
Deny their own kin in the outcast in gray.

Well, take what you will,—though it be on the sly,
Marauding, or begging,—I shall not ask why;
But will call it a dole, just to help on his way
A four-footed friar in orders of gray!

BRET HARTE

GRIZZLY

*C*oward,—of heroic size,
In whose lazy muscles lies
Strength we fear and yet despise;
Savage,—whose relentless tusks
Are content with acorn husks;
Robber,—whose exploits ne'er soared
O'er the bee's or squirrel's hoard;
Whiskered chin and feeble nose,
Claws of steel on baby toes,—
Here, in solitude and shade,
Shambling, shuffling plantigrade,
Be thy courses undismayed!

Here, where Nature makes thy bed,
Let thy rude, half-human tread
    Point to hidden Indian springs,
Lost in ferns and fragrant grasses,
    Hovered o'er by timid wings,
Where the wood-duck lightly passes,
Where the wild bee holds her sweets,—
Epicurean retreats,
Fit for thee, and better than
Fearful spoils of dangerous man.
In thy fat-jowled deviltry
Friar Tuck shall live in thee;

Thou mayst levy tithe and dole;
    Thou shalt spread the woodland cheer,
From the pilgrim taking toll;
    Match thy cunning with his fear;
Eat, and drink, and have thy fill;
Yet remain an outlaw still!

BRET HARTE

THE TIGER

*T*iger! Tiger! burning bright,
In the forests of the night,
What immortal hand or eye
Could frame thy fearful symmetry?

In what distant deeps or skies
Burnt the fire of thine eyes?
On what wings dare he aspire?
What the hand dare seize the fire?

And what shoulder, and what art,
Could twist the sinews of thy heart?
And when thy heart began to beat,
What dread hand and what dread feet?

What the hammer? what the chain?
In what furnace was thy brain?
What the anvil? what dread grasp
Dare its deadly terrors clasp?

When the stars threw down their spears,
And watered heaven with their tears,
Did He smile His work to see?
Did He who made the Lamb, make thee?

Tiger! Tiger! burning bright,
In the forests of the night,
What immortal hand or eye
Dare frame thy fearful symmetry?

WILLIAM BLAKE

THE BLIND MEN AND THE ELEPHANT

*I*t was six men of Indostan
　　To learning much inclined,
Who went to see the elephant
　　(Though all of them were blind),
That each by observation
　　Might satisfy his mind.

The First approached the elephant,
　　And, happening to fall
Against his broad and sturdy side,
　　At once began to bawl:
"God bless me! but the elephant
　　Is nothing but a wall!"

The Second, feeling of the tusk,
　　Cried: "Ho! what have we here
So very round and smooth and sharp?
　　To me 'tis mightly clear
This wonder of an elephant
　　Is very like a spear!"

The Third approached the animal,
　　And, happening to take
The squirming trunk within his hands,
　　Thus boldly up and spake:
"I see," quoth he, "the elephant
　　Is very like a snake!"

The Fourth reached out his eager hand,
   And felt about the knee:
"What most this wondrous beast is like
   Is mighty plain," quoth he;
" 'Tis clear enough the elephant
   Is very like a tree."

The Fifth, who chanced to touch the ear,
   Said: "E'en the blindest man
Can tell what this resembles most;
   Deny the fact who can,
This marvel of an elephant
   Is very like a fan!"

The Sixth no sooner had begun
   About the beast to grope,
Than, seizing on the swinging tail
   That fell within his scope,
"I see," quoth he, "the elephant
   Is very like a rope!"

And so these men of Indostan
   Disputed loud and long,
Each in his own opinion
   Exceeding stiff and strong,
Though each was partly in the right,
   And all were in the wrong!

So, oft in theologic wars
   The disputants, I ween,
Rail on in utter ignorance
   Of what each other mean,
And prate about an elephant
   Not one of them has seen!

JOHN GODFREY SAXE

THE COPPERHEAD

*T*here is peace in the swamp where the Copperhead sleeps,
Where the waters are stagnant, the white vapor creeps,
Where the musk of Magnolia hangs thick in the air,
And the lilies' phylacteries broaden in prayer.
There is peace in the swamp, though the quiet is death,
Though the mist is miasma, the upas-tree's breath,
Though no echo awakes to the cooing of doves,—
There is peace: yes, the peace that the Copperhead loves!

Go seek him: he coils in the ooze and the drip,
Like a thong idly flung from the slave-driver's whip;
But beware the false footstep,—the stumble that brings
A deadlier lash than the overseer swings.
Never arrow so true, never bullet so dread,
As the straight steady stroke of that hammer-shaped head;
Whether slave or proud panther, who braves that dull crest,
Woe to him who shall trouble the Copperhead's rest!

Then why waste your labors, brave hearts and strong men,
In tracking a trail to the Copperhead's den?
Lay your axe to the cypress, hew open the shade
To the free sky and sunshine Jehovah has made;
Let the breeze of the North sweep the vapors away,
Till the stagnant lake ripples, the freed waters play;
And then to your heel can you righteously doom
The Copperhead born of its shadow and gloom!

BRET HARTE

THE SNAKE

A narrow fellow in the grass
Occasionally rides;
You may have met him,—did you not,
His notice sudden is.

The grass divides as with a comb,
A spotted shaft is seen;
And then it closes at your feet
And opens further on.

He likes a boggy acre,
A floor too cool for corn.
Yet when a child, and barefoot,
I more than once, at morn,

Have passed, I thought, a whip-lash
Unbraiding in the sun,—
When, stooping to secure it,
It wrinkled, and was gone.

Several of nature's people
I know, and they know me;
I feel for them a transport
Of cordiality;

But never met this fellow,
Attended or alone,
Without a tighter breathing,
And zero at the bone.

EMILY DICKINSON

THE CROCODILE

*H*ow doth the little crocodile
  Improve his shining tail,
And pour the waters of the Nile
  On every golden scale!

How cheerfully he seems to grin,
  How neatly spreads his claws,
And welcomes little fishes in,
  With gently smiling jaws!

LEWIS CARROLL

THE MALDIVE SHARK

*A*bout the Shark, phlegmatical one,
Pale sot of the Maldive sea,
The sleek little pilot-fish, azure and slim,
How alert in attendance be.
From his saw-pit of mouth, from his charnel of maw
They have nothing of harm to dread,
But liquidly glide on his ghastly flank
Or before his Gorgonian head;
Or lurk in the port of serrated teeth
In white triple tiers of glittering gates,
And there find a haven when peril's abroad,
An asylum in jaws of the Fates!
They are friends; and friendly they guide him to prey,
Yet never partake of the treat—
Eyes and brains to the dotard lethargic and dull,
Pale ravener of horrible meat.

HERMAN MELVILLE

THE HOUSEKEEPER

*T*he frugal snail, with forecast of repose,
Carries his house with him where'er he goes;
Peeps out,—and if there comes a shower of rain,
Retreats to his small domicile amain.
Touch but a tip of him, a horn,—'tis well,—
He curls up in his sanctuary shell.
He's his own landlord, his own tenant; stay
Long as he will, he dreads no Quarter Day.
Himself he boards and lodges; both invites
And feasts himself; sleeps with himself o' nights.
He spares the upholsterer trouble to procure
Chattels; himself is his own furniture,
And his sole riches. Whereso'er he roam,—
Knock when you will,—he's sure to be at home.

CHARLES LAMB

SONNET TO A CLAM

Dum tacent clamant

*I*nglorious friend! most confident I am
   Thy life is one of very little ease;
   Albeit men mock thee with their similes
And prate of being "happy as a clam!"
What though thy shell protects thy fragile head
   From the sharp bailiffs of the briny sea?
   Thy valves are, sure, no safety-valves to thee,
While rakes are free to desecrate thy bed,
And bear thee off—as foemen take their spoil—
   Far from thy friends and family to roam;
   Forced, like a Hessian, from thy native home,
To meet destruction in a foreign broil!
   Though thou art tender yet thy humble bard
   Declares, O clam! thy case is shocking hard!

JOHN GODFREY SAXE

THE CHAMBERED NAUTILUS

*T*his is the ship of pearl, which, poets feign,
  Sail the unshadowed main,—
  The venturous bark that flings
On the sweet summer wind its purpled wings
In gulfs enchanted, where the Siren sings,
  And coral reefs lie bare,
Where the cold sea-maids rise to sun their streaming hair.

Its webs of living gauze no more unfurl;
  Wrecked is the ship of pearl!
  And every chambered cell,
Where its dim dreaming life was wont to dwell,
As the frail tenant shaped his growing shell,
  Before thee lies revealed,—
Its irised ceiling rent, its sunless crypt unsealed!

Year after year beheld the silent toil
    That spread his lustrous coil;
    Still, as the spiral grew,
He left the past year's dwelling for the new,
Stole with soft step its shining archway through,
    Built up its idle door,
Stretched in his last-found home, and knew the old no more.

Thanks for the heavenly message brought by thee,
    Child of the wandering sea,
    Cast from her lap, forlorn!
From thy dead lips a clearer note is born
Than ever Triton blew from wreathéd horn!
    While on mine ear it rings,
Through the deep caves of thought I hear a voice that sings:—

Build thee more stately mansions, O my soul,
    As the swift seasons roll!
    Leave thy low-vaulted past!
Let each new temple, nobler than the last,
Shut thee from heaven with a dome more vast,
    Till thou at length art free,
Leaving thine outgrown shell by life's unresting sea!

OLIVER WENDELL HOLMES

TO A SEABIRD

*S*auntering hither on listless wings,
   Careless vagabond of the sea,
Little thou heedest the surf that sings,
The bar that thunders, the shale that rings,—
   Give me to keep thy company.

Little thou hast, old friend, that's new,
   Storms and wrecks are old things to thee;
Sick am I of these changes, too;
Little to care for, little to rue,—
   I on the shore, and thou on the sea.

All of thy wanderings, far and near,
   Bring thee at last to shore and me;
All of my journeyings end them here,
This our tether must be our cheer,—
   I on the shore, and thou on the sea.

Lazily rocking on ocean's breast,
   Something in common, old friend, have we;
Thou on the shingle seek'st thy nest,
I to the waters look for rest,—
   I on the shore, and thou on the sea.

BRET HARTE

THE SWALLOW

*T*he gorse is yellow on the heath,
　　The banks with speedwell flowers are gay,
The oaks are budding; and beneath,
The hawthorn soon will bear the wreath,
　　The silver wreath of May.

The welcome guest of settled spring,
　　The swallow too is come at last;
Just at sunset, when thrushes sing,
I saw her dash with rapid wing,
　　And hailed her as she passed.

Come, summer visitant, attach
　　To my reed-roof your nest of clay,
And let my ear your music catch,
Low twittering underneath the thatch,
　　At the gray dawn of day.

As fables tell, an Indian sage,
　　The Hindustani woods among,
Could in his desert hermitage,
As if 't were marked in written page,
　　Translate the wild bird's song.

I wish I did his power possess,
　　That I might learn, fleet bird, from thee,
What our vain systems only guess,
And know from what wild wilderness
　　You came across the sea.

CHARLOTTE SMITH

THE EAGLE

*H*e clasps the crag with crooked hands;
Close to the sun in lonely lands,
Ringed with the azure world, he stands.

The wrinkled sea beneath him crawls;
He watches from his mountain walls,
And like a thunderbolt he falls.

ALFRED, LORD TENNYSON

TO THE SKYLARK

Ethereal minstrel! pilgrim of the sky!
　　Dost thou despise the earth where cares abound;
Or, while the wings aspire, are heart and eye
　　Both with thy nest upon the dewy ground?
Thy nest, which thou canst drop into at will
Those quivering wings composed, that music still.

To the last point of vision, and beyond,
　　Mount, daring warbler!—that love-prompted strain,
'Twixt thee and thine a never-failing bond
　　Thrills not the less the bosom of the plain;
Yet mightst thou seem, proud privilege! to sing
All independent of the leafy spring.

Leave to the nightingale her shady wood;
　　A privacy of glorious light is thine,
Whence thou dost pour upon the world a flood
　　Of harmony, with instinct more divine;
Type of the wise, who soar, but never roam,—
True to the kindred points of Heaven and Home.

WILLIAM WORDSWORTH

THE BELFRY PIGEON

*O*n the cross-beam under the Old South bell
The nest of a pigeon is builded well.
In summer and winter that bird is there,
Out and in with the morning air;
I love to see him track the street,
With his wary eye and active feet;
And I often watch him as he springs,
Circling the steeple with easy wings,
Till across the dial his shade has passed,
And the belfry edge is gained at last;
'T is a bird I love, with its brooding note,
And the trembling throb in its mottled throat;
There's a human look in its swelling breast,
And the gentle curve of its lowly crest;
And I often stop with the fear I feel,—
He runs so close to the rapid wheel.

Whatever is rung on that noisy bell,—
Chime of the hour, or funeral knell,—
The dove in the belfry must hear it well.

When the tongue swings out to the midnight moon,
When the sexton cheerly rings for noon,
When the clock strikes clear at morning light,
When the child is waked with "nine at night,"
When the chimes play soft in the Sabbath air,
Filling the spirit with tones of prayer,—
Whatever tale in the bell is heard,
He broods on his folded feet unstirred,
Or, rising half in his rounded nest,
He takes the time to smooth his breast,
Then drops again, with filméd eyes,
And sleeps as the last vibration dies.

   Sweet bird! I would that I could be
A hermit in the crowd like thee!
With wings to fly to wood and glen,
Thy lot, like mine, is cast with men;
And daily, with unwilling feet,
I tread, like thee, the crowded street,
But, unlike me, when day is o'er,
Thou canst dismiss the world, and soar;
Or, at a half-felt wish for rest,
Canst smooth the feathers on thy breast,
And drop, forgetful, to thy nest.

   I would that in such wings of gold
I could my weary heart upfold;
I would I could look down unmoved
(Unloving as I am unloved),
And while the world throngs on beneath,
Smooth down my cares and calmly breathe;
And never sad with others' sadness,
And never glad with others' gladness,
Listen, unstirred, to knell or chime,
And, lapped in quiet, bide my time.

NATHANIEL PARKER WILLIS

THE ROBIN

*T*he robin is the one
That interrupts the morn
With hurried, few, express reports
When March is scarcely on.

The robin is the one
That overflows the noon
With her cherubic quantity,
An April but begun.

The robin is the one
That speechless from her nest
Submits that home and certainty
And sanctity are best.

EMILY DICKINSON

THE BLUEBIRD

*B*efore you thought of spring,
Except as a surmise,
You see, God bless his suddenness,
A fellow in the skies
Of independent hues,
A little weather-worn,
Inspiriting habiliments
Of indigo and brown.

With specimens of song,
As if for you to choose,
Discretion in the interval,
With gay delays he goes
To some superior tree
Without a single leaf,
And shouts for joy to nobody
But his seraphic self!

EMILY DICKINSON

THE OWL

*I*n the hollow tree, in the old gray tower,
   The spectral owl doth dwell;
Dull, hated, despised, in the sunshine hour,
   But at dusk he's abroad and well!
Not a bird of the forest e'er mates with him;
   All mock him outright by day;
But at night, when the woods grow still and dim,
   The boldest will shrink away!
     O, when the night falls, and roosts the fowl,
     Then, then, *is the reign of the horned owl!*

And the owl hath a bride, who is fond and bold,
   And loveth the wood's deep gloom;
And, with eyes like the shine of the moonstone cold,
   She awaiteth her ghastly groom;
Not a feather she moves, not a carol she sings,
   As she waits in her tree so still;
But when her heart heareth his flapping wings,
   She hoots out her welcome shrill!
     O, when the moon shines, and dogs do howl,
     Then, then, *is the joy of the horned owl!*

Mourn not for the owl, nor his gloomy plight!
   The owl hath his share of good:
If a prisoner he be in the broad daylight,
   He is lord in the dark greenwood!
Nor lonely the bird, nor his ghastly mate,
   They are each unto each a pride;
Thrice fonder, perhaps, since a strange, dark fate
   Hath rent them from all beside!
     So, when the night falls, and dogs do howl,
     Sing, ho! for the reign of the horned owl!
       We know not always
       Who are kings by day,
     But the king of the night is the bold brown owl!

BARRY CORNWALL

TO THE CUCKOO

O blithe New-comer! I have heard,
    I hear thee and rejoice.
O Cuckoo! shall I call thee Bird,
    Or but a wand'ring Voice?

While I am lying on the grass
    Thy twofold shout I hear;
From hill to hill it seems to pass,
    At once far off, and near.

Though babbling only to the Vale
    Of sunshine and of flowers,
Thou bringest unto me a tale
    Of visionary hours.

Thrice welcome, darling of the Spring!
    Even yet thou art to me
No bird, but an invisible thing,
    A voice, a mystery;

The same whom in my school-boy days
   I listened to; that Cry
Which made me look a thousand ways,
   In bush, and tree, and sky.

To seek thee did I often rove
   Through woods and on the green;
And thou wert still a hope, a love;
   Still longed for, never seen

And I can listen to thee yet;
   Can lie upon the plain
And listen, till I do beget
   That golden time again.

O blessed Bird! the earth we pace
   Again appears to be
An unsubstantial, faery place;
   That is fit home for Thee!

WILLIAM WORDSWORTH

TO THE CANARY-BIRD

I cannot hear thy voice with others' ears,
Who make of thy lost liberty a gain;
And in thy tale of blighted hopes and fears
Feel not that every note is born with pain.
Alas! that with thy music's gentle swell
Past days of joy should through thy memory throng,
And each to thee their words of sorrow tell,
While ravish'd sense forgets thee in thy song.
The heart that on the past and future feeds,
And pours in human words its thoughts divine,
Though at each birth the spirit inly bleeds,
Its song may charm the listening ear like thine,
And men with gilded cage and praise will try
To make the bard, like thee, forget his native sky.

JONES VERY

THE MOCKING BIRD

At Night

A golden pallor of voluptuous light
Filled the warm southern night:
The moon, clear orbed, above the sylvan scene
Moved like a stately queen,
So rife with conscious beauty all the while,
What could she do but smile
At her own perfect loveliness below,
Glassed in the tranquil flow
Of crystal fountains and unruffled streams?
Half lost in waking dreams,
As down the loneliest forest dell I strayed,
Lo! from a neighboring glade,
Flashed through the drifts of moonshine, swiftly came
A fairy shape of flame.
It rose in dazzling spirals overhead,
Whence to wild sweetness wed,
Poured marvelous melodies, silvery trill on trill;
The very leaves grew still
On the charmed trees to hearken; while for me,
Heart-trilled to ecstasy,
I followed—followed the bright shape that flew,
Still circling up the blue,
Till as a fountain that has reached its height,
Falls back in sprays of light
Slowly dissolved, so that enrapturing lay,
Divinely melts away
Through tremulous spaces to a music-mist,
Soon by the fitful breeze
How gently kissed
Into remote and tender silences.

PAUL HAMILTON HAYNE

ALL THINGS BRIGHT AND BEAUTIFUL

*A*ll things bright and beautiful,
All creatures great and small,
All things wise and wonderful,
The Lord God made them all.

CECIL FRANCES ALEXANDER